Velazq

S. L. Bensusan

Alpha Editions

This edition published in 2024

ISBN : 9789362929280

Design and Setting By
Alpha Editions
www.alphaedis.com
Email - info@alphaedis.com

Contents

INTRODUCTION

It is a curious truth that Spain in these days of her decline exercises almost as much control over the mind of the world as she exercised over its territories in the days of her great empire. Cervantes in literature and Velazquez in art seem destined to secure for their country a measure of immortality that throws into the background the memory of such people as Carlos Quinto, Philip II., and those other lesser lights who made the name of Spain respected or detested throughout Europe and South America. If science and art are destined, as some altruists hope, to unite the world in a bond that defies the arbitrary boundaries made by rulers, then the name of Diego de Silva Velazquez will stand high in the list of those whom the world delights to honour, for people who are opposed diametrically on all questions of politics and faith find ground upon which they may meet in security and amity when they stand before the pictures of the great Spanish master. And Cervantes, who used words instead of colours to express the life he saw around him, would redeem Spain from insignificance if she had never owned a colony, and had never sought to step beyond her own borders to develop the arts of peace or follow the paths of war.

Perhaps it would be hard to find more diverse opinions than those that are heard in the studio. Artists see life through the medium of many temperaments, they are notoriously intemperate in their enthusiasms. There are schools of painting to suit every conviction, and the work that one man would give his all to possess would not find hanging space upon the wall controlled by another. But before Velazquez even artists forget their controversies; he stands, like Bach and Beethoven in the world of music, respected even by those who do not understand. No controversy rages round him; he has marched unchallenged to the highest place in men's regard.

PLATE II.—LAS MENIÑAS

This picture was painted about the year 1656, and, now in the Prado, is considered one of the greatest works of the master. It presents the Infanta Margarita attended by her maids of honour, while Velazquez himself is shown painting the portraits of Philip IV. and his second wife Mariana of Austria, who are seen reflected in the mirror.

It is interesting to note that a reputation unrivalled in the world of pictures is founded upon a comparatively small number of works. One of his latest critics reduces the pictures of Velazquez now in existence to eighty-nine, while acknowledging that some have disappeared from the royal palaces of Spain and cannot be traced. This critic, Señor Don Aureliano de Beruete—a connoisseur, a collector, and a worker in the best interests of art—is perhaps a little too severe. He will not admit to his catalogue a portrait like that of Admiral Adriano Pulido Pareja, which, despite some inferior workmanship, can show considerable claims to be regarded as genuine; but even if all the disputed ones were admitted, and such a list as the late R. A. M. Stevenson published were accepted without that far-seeing critic's own reserve, we should not have as many pictures to represent the forty years of the artist's life as Sir Joshua Reynolds was known to paint in a single year. Velazquez has left very few drawings, and these are of small importance; there are but two acknowledged engravings; and to limit still further our sources of knowledge, the artist's correspondence seems to have been lost; while the Memoirs which Velazquez was said to have drawn up when Philip IV. sent the pictures to the Escorial are now admitted by the best authorities to be the work of another man.

I
THE METHOD AND INFLUENCE OF VELAZQUEZ

In dealing with the life and work of the Spanish master, even in the modest fashion of this little monograph, one must bear in mind the fact that Velazquez, in the eyes of his contemporaries, was not only an artist—he was a court painter; and pictures other than portraits were of comparatively little importance to Philip IV. and his circle. Art borrowed most of her importance in sixteenth and seventeenth century Spain from the fact that she was the handmaid of Holy Mother Church. Velazquez was a court official who chanced to be a clever portrait-painter, and his promotion tended ever to take him further away from his art. With the increase of state duties the claims upon his time grew more and more difficult to meet, and, when he rose in the closing years of his life to be Grand Marshal of the Palace, entrusted with the ordering of state functions and missions to distinguished foreigners, his art became entirely a secondary consideration. The studio was no more than a place of refuge for the artist in the hours when he might forget that he was an official. If Velazquez had not been compelled to sacrifice the best part of forty years' activity to the ridiculous formalities of court life, the world might have been richer to-day by scores of pictures worthy to rank by the side of "Las Meniñas" and the portrait of Pope Innocent X. The painter might have found outside court circles far more inspiring sitters than those whom he was compelled to paint, for it takes all that even a Velazquez can give to a portrait to make a Philip IV., a Mariana of Austria, or even an Isabella of Bourbon, reveal their dominant characteristics without caricature; indeed one feels that the interest belongs to the picture and not to the sitter. The success is one of tone, of harmony and of line, of sure handling directed by an inward vision.

Because of gifts lying beyond praise, the painter has preserved seventeenth-century Spain for us as far as court circles represent it; but among the many charges laid to the account of Philip IV. must be added that of limiting the range and crippling the capacity of an artist who cannot be placed second to any man.

When we come to analyse his work we find that its qualities are not of a sensational kind. Velazquez makes no appeal through the medium of brilliant pigment; his great contemporary Rubens used colour in far more striking fashion. Velazquez loved grey and silvery tints, and in the years of his maturity understood relative values perfectly. He knew, too, exactly how far he could go, and never made experiments in search of qualities that were not his. Although he had a certain quality of delicate imagination, he was a realist, and could not paint without a model; he never acquired a mannerism, or applied to one sitter the treatment that some artists seem to keep for types. Every figure he set upon canvas has its own individuality, and, while Velazquez, like other artists, had manners and methods that belong to fixed periods of his life, it is not easy to set down in cold print an analysis of the causes that make up his effects. He had no tricks; everything that he did was clear, simple, and withal inimitable. Hundreds of men have copied his pictures; none has been able to copy his method. With his death his influence upon art ceased. His genius lay buried in the grave with him, and did not suffer complete resurrection until the nineteenth century was turning towards its successor, though Raphael Mengs had done all he could to make his merits known a hundred years before. Even to-day, we may be said to be in the first stage of our enjoyment of the master's work. There are at least fifty good books upon the subject of Velazquez' life and art, written in three or four languages, and all published in the last half century; there must be many more to come, for every generation sees genius in the light of its own time.

So much for literature. In art the painter has influenced very many moderns. Manet, Courbet, Corot, Millet, Whistler, are among the men whose work shines in the light of the Prado, and the list might be prolonged indefinitely, for all earnest art workers go to Velazquez, confident that whatever their aims and ideals, he will confirm and strengthen what is best in them. They know, too, that they may return again and again, and that the rich stores of guidance and encouragement in the pursuit of ideals are as inexhaustible as the barrel of meal that did not waste, and the cruse of oil that did not fail, in the house of the widow of Zarephath.

II
THE PAINTER'S EARLY DAYS

In the years when Velazquez first saw the light, the power of Spain, despite the shock it had received from British seamen, was the dominating factor in European politics. Philip II. had come to the end of a reign of more than forty years; Philip III. had just reached the throne. The painter was not born in the atmosphere of court life, but in the very Catholic city of Seville, then as now a fatal place for those who cannot withstand the manifold temptations to lead a lazy life. Happily for the boy his parents had not inherited the Seville traditions; his father came from Oporto, which, being a seaport town, has no lack of mental and physical activity. The spirit of painting settled at a very early age upon young Diego de Silva Velazquez— the second name by which he is universally known belonged to his mother's family—almost before he was in his teens he was working in the studio of Francisco de Herrera, architect and painter. The temperaments of master and pupil could not fuse; there was sufficient trouble to lead Don Juan Rodriguez to transfer his son's services to Francesco Pacheco, painter, poet, professor, and withal a man of action and experience. He knew much about contemporary art, encouraged a hopeful outlook upon life, and enjoyed the respect of all men. Moreover his studio was the meeting-place for many of the distinguished folk of the city. In the very early years of their association Pacheco understood that his young pupil was not like other lads, that he possessed an individuality that could not be repressed or directed into the usual channels, and instead of resenting this new element, he sought to direct it wisely and kindly, thereby laying Velazquez under a debt of gratitude that the painter never repudiated. Indeed there were stronger ties in the making, for in the spring of 1618, when the young artist was on the threshold of his wonderful career, Pacheco gave him his daughter Juana for wife, "encouraged," he says, "by his virtues, his fine qualities, and the hopes which his happy nature and great talent raised in me." The kind old painter is not remembered to-day by his pictures, or even by his "Book of Portraits of Illustrious Personages," and other quaintly titled works from his pen. He lives because he helped to make Velazquez a great painter, and recorded his impression of his son-in-law's earliest works, the various "Bodegones," of which several may be seen in London to-day. Others are in Berlin and St. Petersburg. From these pictures of the secular life Velazquez passed to religious subjects—"Christ in the House of Martha" (National Gallery) and the "Adoration of the Magi" (Prado) belong to these early years.

PLATE III.—THE INFANTE PHILIP PROSPER

This picture hangs in the Imperial Gallery of Vienna. It is the work of the painter's last period, and shows us the little son of Philip IV. by his second wife. The lad died some two years after the picture was painted; it has been restored, not too cleverly.

In 1622, Velazquez, already the father of two children, made his first journey to Madrid, and was allowed to visit the royal palaces. He did not stay long in Castile, and his return to the capital was brought about by the divinity that shapes men's ends. Philip III. was dead; his son Philip IV. had selected as friend and adviser the Count Olivarez, son of the Governor of the Alcazar in Seville. Olivarez had many friends in the city that wears the "Modo" for its badge, in recognition of unswerving loyalty to Alfonso the Learned. Doubtless he had heard about the work of the young painter and had seen some examples of it, and he wished to strengthen himself in the capital by bringing accomplished men from his own city to official posts in Madrid. So he sent for Velazquez, who journeyed a second time to the north, now in the company of Pacheco, and on arrival there painted a lost portrait of a Gentleman Usher, Fonseca by name. This picture did for Velazquez what the portrait of Admiral Keppel did for Reynolds, and before the excitement died away, the young King Philip IV. had deigned to promise a sitting to the clever Sevillian. The success of the first picture of Philip IV. (apparently the early one now in the Prado) was so complete that the king ordered all existing portraits of himself to be removed from the palace, and gave the painter an order of admission to his service with a salary of about two pounds five shillings a month! Under the skilled hands of the artist we are permitted to see the tall, gloomy lad grow up a dull, reserved man, and we read in his face a part at least of the causes of Spain's ultimate downfall.

III
VELAZQUEZ IN MADRID

Of the painter's work at court in those early days we hear a little from Pacheco, but the story of the times is more or less obscure. A clever portrait-painter was not a very interesting person in the eyes of a Spanish grandee. He was classed with the court buffoons and dwarfs who existed merely to amuse. Indeed, portraiture was not above suspicion in the eyes of some fanatics, who held that art existed to serve the Church, and should not seek secular employment. There are documents extant showing that Velazquez received eight pounds for three portraits, of which one is lost and the other two (Philip and the Count of Olivarez) are in Spain. In 1625 the painter received a present of three hundred ducats, which was followed by a pension of the same value and a gift of free lodging, and, in 1627, by the appointment to the post of Gentleman Usher. There is no doubt but that the king was attached to his young court painter in a certain undemonstrative fashion. Pacheco tells us that Philip used to visit the artist's studio constantly, reaching it by way of the secret passages of which the palace was full.

The year 1628 marks an event of the first importance in the life of Velazquez, for Peter Paul Rubens came on a diplomatic mission to Madrid, charged by his government to pave the way to the conclusion of peace between England and Spain. Rubens was then about fifty years old. He stayed nine months in the Spanish capital, and, despite his diplomatic duties and the gout, found time to paint an extraordinary number of pictures, including five of Philip. He also copied the king's Titians. Velazquez was entrusted by Philip with the work of entertaining Rubens, and showing him the art treasures of Spain, and the friendship that grew up rapidly between the two artists was creditable to both, because Rubens, then at the zenith of his fame, recognised the amazing gifts of the young Spaniard, and Velazquez never allowed the brilliancy of the ambassador-artist to tempt him from the paths that he had chosen to follow. There are some who think that Rubens exerted a great influence upon his young friend's art, but we cannot pretend to trace it. Rubens may have widened his mind; he could not influence his hand or eye.

Shortly after Rubens left Madrid, Velazquez completed his picture "Los Borrachos," now in the Prado, and one of the acknowledged masterpieces of his first style, though the tone is dark, and some of the figures do not blend with their surroundings. In the late summer of the same year Velazquez left Spain for Italy, in the company of Don Ambrosio Spinola, who was going to take command of the Spanish forces. Soldier and artist parted at Milan, and the latter went to Venice, where he stayed with the Spanish ambassador and copied some of Tintoretto's pictures. Thence he went by way of Ferrara to Rome, the honoured guest of a relation of the Count of Olivarez, and he busied himself copying old pictures and painting new ones. Like many of the artists who go for the first time to Italy, he was influenced in some degree by Guido, who was then living. He painted his own portrait, which is to be seen in the Capitoline Museum, and went from Rome to Naples, returning to Madrid in the early part of 1651.

PLATE IV.—THE INFANTE DON BALTHASAR CARLOS

This is one of the Prado pictures of King Philip's eldest son by his first wife, the unfortunate little prince who died while he was yet a boy. When this picture was painted Don Balthasar Carlos was six years old.

It might be mentioned in this place that the painter's eldest daughter was growing up, and that he married her three years later to one of his pupils, the artist J. B. del Mazo. This clever artist, who was treated by his master Velazquez as Velazquez had been treated by his master Pacheco, is held by critics to be responsible for many pictures generally ascribed to his father-in-law. There is a picture in the Wallace Collection known as the "Lady with the Fan," which is thought by no less a critic than Señor Beruete to represent the young Francesca Velazquez, who became the Señora del Mazo when she was only fifteen years old.

Shortly after his return to Madrid, Velazquez came under the influence of El Greco, who had died in 1614, and left some wonderful pictures that may be seen to-day in Toledo. This fact is important, not that the influence resulted in imitation, but because it was distinctly inspiring, and Greco is a painter who is coming slowly before the public. It cannot be doubted that his influence on artists through Velazquez has been very deep and abiding, particularly in portraiture.

In the years following the return from Italy, Velazquez painted some of the pictures of the little prince Don Balthasar Carlos, the king's son, who was born in 1629, and died in 1646, the year of his betrothal to Mariana of Austria. There are many pictures of this interesting lad who, had he lived, might have done so much to save his country. The earliest was painted as soon as Velazquez returned from Italy, and is at present in Boston. The next in date would seem to be the one in the Wallace Collection, and following this comes the well-known picture of Don Balthasar in hunting dress, now in the Prado, the one with the small greyhound seen on the right, just coming into the canvas. Then we have the famous picture of the young prince on his spirited Andalusian pony, which is perhaps the most popular of all; and succeeding that in the order of the painting comes the portrait that, in the writer's opinion, is the best of the series. It hangs in the Imperial Museum in Vienna, and was painted when the prince was about eleven years old. Doubtless there are other portraits of the ill-fated boy, whose features seem to suggest that he had inherited from his mother some of the qualities that his father lacked, and that had he been spared to succeed his father in 1665, he would have handled affairs with vigour and intelligence.

In 1638 Philip's daughter Maria Teresa was born, and the history of the artist's life in Madrid becomes uneventful or lost. Probably on account of the increasing unrest abroad and the decline of the Spanish fortunes, Velazquez' earliest patron, the Count of Olivarez, was disgraced in 1643, the year in which Condé helped to break the power of Spain at Rocroi.

Although the condition of the Spanish Empire was very unfavourable, and Philip IV. must have known long hours of anxiety and unrest, there is no reason to believe that he withdrew his company or his favour from the best beloved of his court painters. Spinola had taken Breda from Justin of Nassau, and the surrender was promptly immortalised by Velazquez in the picture "Las Lanzas," which draws so many pilgrims to Madrid to-day. It was painted for the palace of Buen Retiro, and curiously enough—since it records one of the few successes of Spain in the Low Countries—the subject passed out of men's memory, and for many years nobody knew why the artist had painted it, or what it was all about. Some time between the painting of this picture and the fall of Olivarez, Murillo came to Madrid and became a pupil of Velazquez, who had just received a grant of five hundred ducats to be paid annually by order of the king. In 1644 Velazquez accompanied Philip on a journey through Aragon, and two or three years later he was appointed Inspector of Buildings, a post involving much tedious work, and helping to keep the painter from his studio. He seems to have bestowed a certain amount of labour on portraits painted by other men, in order to bring them into harmony with the collection that Philip was making. It is difficult to deal with this matter within limited space because the details are distinctly controversial, but it is as well to remember that some of the portraits attributed to Velazquez in the Prado Gallery are of people who were dead before Velazquez was painting, so they could not have sat for him; and in the days of Philip IV. it was considered no disgrace for a man to repaint another artist's canvases. Moreover, a painter to the court of Spain was not supposed to carry an uneasy conscience about with him. It was his duty to obey orders and to accept from his superiors as much guidance and direction as they were gracious enough to give him.

In 1649 the king granted Velazquez permission to return to Italy in order to find pictures for a Royal Academy of Fine Art to be established in Madrid. By this time Philip was a widower, though he was on the point of marrying his niece, Mariana of Austria. She had been affianced to the Infante Don Balthasar Carlos, but he had been dead for three years, and the Spanish throne was without an heir. Velazquez visited Genoa, Venice, Milan, and Padua, and brought back pictures by Veronese and Tintoretto. Rome and Naples were revisited, and the famous portrait of Pope Innocent X., of which one copy is in St. Petersburg, and the other in the Doria Palace in Rome, was painted. The former is a bust and a study; the latter is a three-quarter length, and is painted with a wonderful blend of red and white. It was copied by Sir Joshua Reynolds, who declared that it was the finest work he had seen in Rome. What would he have thought of the later masterpieces by the same hand? The portrait was copied by other men too, and there is no doubt that the copies were in some cases sold for originals.

By the time Velazquez returned to Madrid in 1651, at the urgent request of his royal master, the court of Spain was *en fête*. Philip's wife, to whom he had been married two years, was only seventeen, and required amusement. Functions of every sort, excursions, entertainments on a most sumptuous scale, were the order of the day, and because Velazquez was now at the summit of his achievement, because he could paint pictures that will endure as long as men care for art, it is difficult indeed to forgive Philip IV. for making him Marshal of the Palace. To be sure the post was well paid, the salary being about £400 a year with lodging in the Treasure House, but the duties were endless. The king's action was on a par with the custom that prevails in our own Foreign Office, of sending a man who understands China thoroughly to serve the country in Peru, and one who has mastered Russian politics to Portugal.

PLATE V.—ANTONIO THE ENGLISHMAN

This was one of the dwarfs in the service of the king. His is one of the last portraits painted by Velazquez. The figure is life size, and hangs in the Prado at Madrid.

Happily Velazquez, for all that he was regarded in Madrid as a rather lazy man, found time when he was Marshal of the Palace to paint the best of all his portraits. He was honoured by Queen Mariana of Austria, the king's second wife, who sat for him on several occasions, and the results may be seen in Paris, Vienna, New York, and Madrid. Some of the portraits, painted without a suspicion of flattery, show the absurd head-dress, the false hair, and the extraordinary crinoline that were worn at the time, in all their ugliness, and force us to see how great was the distance lying between the royal house and any sense of beauty. Velazquez was not perhaps very happy with this work, because Nature had endowed Philip's wife with a face that was almost as dull and unresponsive to emotion as that of her lord and master; but after a time children were born, and the court painter had a more sympathetic task. He has left portraits that are quite charming of the Infanta Margarita and the Infante Philip Prosper; he painted both of the children while they were very young. In point of fact, neither lived to grow up; doubtless they would have been uninteresting enough if they had been spared. The Infanta Margarita is to be seen in Vienna, in Paris, and in Madrid, and she of course is the centre of the famous picture, "Las Meniñas." Prince Prosper was painted by Velazquez, when no more than two years old. There were two other children, Prince Ferdinand and Prince Carlos II., but the former was no more than a year old when Velazquez died, and Carlos was unborn. Of the four children born to Philip IV. by his second wife, three died young.

In the last years of his life, when the pressure of court duties and the ill-will of highly placed fools must have been hard to bear, Velazquez found time to paint some of his greatest masterpieces. "The Maids of Honour" ("Las Meniñas"), "The Spinners" ("Las Hilanderas"), "Æsop," "Menippus," "The Coronation of the Virgin," and the "Venus with the Mirror," are all the ripe fruit of the painter's last decade. His art had matured; adversity had thrown him back upon his work; it was the solace of the hours that were not claimed by absurd official duties. Who shall say that the scant consideration he received from parasites and courtiers was an unmixed evil? The men who despised the painter because Philip favoured him may have helped to mould his character, may have enabled him to detach himself completely from his own official character when he could lay aside the garb of office and turn to his beloved canvases once again. The portraits of Philip in his last years, those of his second wife and her children, those of the dwarfs too, belong to the years between 1651 and 1660.

It was a custom of the unhealthy and depressing Spanish court in which the queen lived in an armour of corsets and crinoline, and might not be touched by any of her faithful subjects upon pain of death—the court in which the king was compelled to preside at the *autos da fé*—to keep dwarfs as playthings.

Perhaps because they were ugly and deformed they came quite naturally into the court environment. The earliest portrait of Don Balthasar Carlos shows him in company with a dwarf, and there were about the court many other unfortunate creatures whom Velazquez painted between 1650 and 1659.

There is more than a suspicion in the minds of many of his biographers that the half-concealed contempt with which Velazquez was regarded in court circles left him small choice of company; that he was rated with dwarfs and outcasts because he worked with his hands; and of course no hidalgo, who was a perfect master of the art of time-wasting, could take seriously any low-blooded creature who earned his right to live by working. If Velazquez had been on the same footing as Rubens—had he enjoyed the same position that Goya, with no greater official appointment, was to hold a little more than a century after his death—we may presume that the dwarfs would not have been painted, and that Velazquez' art would have been given to the service of the blue-blooded gentlemen who were making as big a muddle of Spanish interests as their country's worst enemies could desire. One hesitates to say that they would have been less interesting sitters, because we know that nobody, however dull and stupid in appearance, could fail to become interesting at the hands of the painter. It is fair to remember, too, in defence of the Spanish attitude, that the years were given not to the arts of peace but to those of war; that leisure was scanty, intrigue unceasing, and the austerity of life was made greater by the strong and merciless grip of the Church. Formality and superstition marched hand in hand in a court whose ruler, if we may judge by his portraits, had forgotten how to smile. Then again, the atmosphere of the Madrid court, for all its dulness and secrecy and unhealthy ways, was not as it became under Charles III., when Godoy played the part of Count Olivarez, and the Countess Benavente, the Duchess of Alba, and other women as frail as they were beautiful, did not hesitate to indulge in open intrigue with the king's painter. Turn to the canvases of Velazquez and you will not find a woman who was fascinating enough to have been worth the trouble and danger of an intrigue. The wives of Philip IV. could not but have been virtuous, and would have had but small sympathy with pretty women. To be sure Philip IV. had many mistresses, but he did not ask his court painter to record their beauty.

Before Velazquez returned to Madrid from his second visit to Italy, he seems to have painted the portrait of the dwarf known as "El Primo," now in the Prado. This man, known in private life as Don Louis de Hacedo, accompanied Philip on a tour, and he seems to have been a studious person, because the artist has depicted him with book, pen, and paper, and given him a refined expression. The others have little to redeem their ugliness and deformity. The child of Vallecas seems to be the dwarf who figures with Don Balthasar Carlos in the first picture that Velazquez painted of the unfortunate young prince, the one that is now in America. He has grown a little older and a little more ugly in the canvas that is devoted entirely to his portrait; he does not wear good clothes, but a coarse green coat with stockings to match. The Idiot of Coria is also dressed in green, though his garments are a little richer, but Don Antonio seems to have been a person of some importance. He is pictured in the Prado standing beside a beautiful mastiff almost as big as himself, and he wears a ruddy brown dress worked with gold. He carries a large plumed hat in his hand. Sebastian de Morra, who sits facing the audience, has one of the most wonderful heads ever set on canvas by the artist. This dwarf too is dressed in the green costume that would seem to have been worn by the dwarfs attached to the court of Spain. In addition to the little company of dwarfs there were buffoons at the court, and of these Velazquez painted Pablillos, who is known as "the comedian," and Don Juan of Austria, whose portrait is a triumph of harmony in colour, the pink of mantle and stockings contrasting admirably with black doublet and cape.

PLATE VI.—ADMIRAL ADRIANO PULIDO PAREJA

This picture may be seen in the National Gallery. It is signed and dated 1639, and was purchased from the Longford Castle Collection in 1890. Señor Beruete holds a strong opinion that it was not painted by Velazquez.

In the last years the painter seems to have gone a little further down in the social scale in search of his sitters, for the "Æsop" is a beggar, and "Menippus" is no better. To all these sufferers and outcasts Velazquez responded with a sympathy that is not less clearly revealed than the technique that gives so much enduring delight to artists the world over.

In the final decade of the painter's life Philip seems to have given him no more than two sittings. Perhaps the artist's "Mars" and his "Venus with the Mirror" gave offence in Madrid, where the nude was only accepted if it was painted by some artist who had won his fame outside the Iberian Peninsula. The whole trend of life in the court of Mariana of Austria was opposed to the presentation of the nude in art. The two late pictures of Philip, of which the one is in the Prado and the second in our National Gallery, are quite the most finished of all his studies of his royal master. The face, free from even a suggestion of human interest or enthusiasm, has no emotion whatsoever save disillusionment and sadness. The spectator gets a suggestion that life has resolved itself into a long series of formal duties and formal enjoyments, and that neither suffices to make it worth living. Duty to the world at large and to the vast empire slipping from his grasp seems to be all that holds Philip; and when we consider that he had lost his first wife and her promising son, and of his children by his second wife one or two were dead already; that dissipation and anxiety had sapped his energies, and superstition had crabbed his intelligence; it is not strange that the face should be as it is.

In 1658 Philip conferred upon Velazquez the knighthood of Santiago, and money was deposited on his behalf by a friend who understood the painter's financial straits to pay for the inquiries relating to his genealogy. In spite of the king's wishes, the Council appointed to inquire into the antecedents of the painter refused to admit him, though Velazquez supplied many proofs that his blood was pure and his origin honourable. At last, Philip applied to the Pope Alexander VII. for a dispensation in the artist's favour, realising that the Vatican was a Court whose jurisdiction was unlimited in its scope. The Pope was complaisant: he could hardly be otherwise to Philip IV.; he sent a brief that enabled Velazquez, after long delays, to obtain the much coveted order. The story that Philip bestowed it upon Velazquez as a reward for the picture "Las Meniñas" is one of the pretty fables that must be disregarded, and it seems likely that Philip only exerted himself on his painter's behalf because he wished him to superintend the arrangements for the festivities that were to celebrate the marriage of the Infanta Maria Teresa with Louis XIV. If we may read character in physiognomy, there is little risk that Philip would have behaved generously without cause.

Velazquez left Madrid for Irun, on the Franco-Spanish frontier, in April 1660. The work was harassing; he was not a *persona grata* with his colleagues, and none sought to lighten his burdens. He returned to the capital at the end of June, when Madrid is not fit to live in, and was taken ill a month later. Hard and unremitting labour, the folly and bitter opposition of men who were not worthy to clean his palette, the inconveniences and delays of travel in Spain, and the tender mercies of several Spanish doctors of repute, seem to have combined, with a bad attack of fever, to bring a troubled life to its closing scene. The end came on the 6th of August 1660, when, to quote Señor Beruete, "he delivered up his soul to God, who had created him to be the admiration of the world."

The body was decorated with the ornaments of the knights of Santiago and buried in the parish church of St. John the Baptist. Within a week his devoted wife, Juana de Pacheco Velazquez, followed him to a rest that no ceremonial of the Spanish court could disturb.

Strange as it may seem to those who know nothing of Spain, the petty worries and vexations to which Velazquez had been subjected did not cease with his death. It was decided by the authorities that the thousand ducats paid to the dead painter for superintending the works of the Alcazar must be returned, and in order that the claim might be met, the contents of the artist's studio and some of his furniture would seem to have been seized. King Philip recorded his gracious distress at this decision, but did nothing to overrule it.

Litigation followed, and after some years the claim to the thousand ducats was withdrawn by the authorities, the affairs of the master were wound up for all time, and the stigma of debt was removed from the memory of a man who never received a tithe of his deserts.

Philip IV. took Juan del Mazo, the painter's son-in-law, to be court painter in Velazquez' place, and the appointment is worth noting, because it is to this worthy man's wonderful facility for echoing his father-in-law's style that we owe the presence of so many imitations in the world's public galleries and private collections. Some of these clever copies of lost pictures have remained unchallenged until recent years, and whether this be a tribute to the capacity of del Mazo or a reflection upon the capacity of critics, is a question lying beyond the scope of this little book. But it is not difficult to understand that the renown of Velazquez was on the increase for a few years after his death, and that Mazo, who was clever and poorly paid, and had a sincere respect for his father-in-law, should have remembered that there is no greater flattery than imitation.

IV
A RETROSPECT

It is in no spirit of extravagance that one ventures to say that the life of Velazquez was a long and tragic struggle against surroundings detrimental to the full and natural expression of his genius, nor is it surprising that the people who had followed his career with indifference saw very little matter for comment when he died. There were a few useless and pompous ceremonies associated with his obsequies, and Spain went on with the daily task, the common round, unconscious of her loss. So many material possessions were passing from hands too weak to hold or to administer them that the death of an artist could not be noticed.

PLATE VII.—DONNA MARIANA OF AUSTRIA

This picture was brought from the Escorial to the Prado in 1845. The lady was the second wife of Philip IV., and would have been the wife of Don Balthasar Carlos had he lived.

Fair-minded critics may hesitate to say with Spain's enemies that civilisation ends with the Pyrenees, but it is certain that the Spanish attitude towards life has differed from that of other countries to an extent that has left indelible impressions upon art and literature. Velazquez carried a little of the Andalusian sun to Castile, but the heavy cloud that settled upon the Spanish court speedily obscured it. Life for the painter was an affair of constant struggle against financial and social difficulties, of endless work for unresponsive masters; and the labour was not lightened by any of the associations that helped the great masters of the Italian School who had some share of light and honour. The funereal pomp of the Spanish court; the strange climatic conditions of Madrid, where you may pass in a moment from a blaze of sun that scorches to a blast of icy wind that strikes a fatal blow at the lungs; the hard and unattractive landscape; the proud, cruel, and impassive people who cannot even feign an interest in such affairs as art or letters, all served to leave their impression upon the painter's work. We cannot imagine that any artist who worked in Madrid in the seventeenth century could become a colourist after the manner of the Venetians; he would not see the colour unless he went to Catalonia or Andalusia and entered into their stirring national life. Then again Spain was influenced by the Moors, and eastern art is more concerned with harmony than colouring, more concerned to blend neutral tints than present rich tones.

The writer has seen many pictures in the studios of modern Madrid that are inspired directly by the Italians, for nowadays Spanish artists flock to Italy, where they learn to imitate the Venetian colour schemes, and to become third-rate echoes of old masters. There are a few men who paint interesting pictures in Spain to-day—Pradilla and Carbonero are among the best; but Spain does not hold a great artist. The last of all died in exile in Bordeaux in the early days of the last century, and left his gifts to the French School of Manet.

Velazquez could never have become a flamboyant colourist. A few of the pictures in the Prado have some reds and pinks; for example, "Las Hilanderas," in which there is a red curtain, and the picture of Philip on horseback, in which the king wears a pink scarf. There are high colours in "The Coronation of the Virgin" and a few others, but as a rule Velazquez wrought with a subdued palette, and sought to weave harmonies in grey and silver. Bright colours are an expression of the joy of life, and this was unknown to the Spaniards of Castile. Murillo has colour, but then he was always an Andalusian. Just as Velazquez borrowed very little from his sitters and gave a great deal, so he claimed next to nothing from the primary colours, and he gave a colour sense that is indescribably beautiful to silver and grey. This was his deliberate choice and judgment, but it is impossible to forget that surroundings and associations must have had a great deal to do with it. Men who live lives that are complete in the fullest sense of the term have a natural craving for glowing hues, and may find Velazquez dull if they come to the Prado from the Academy of Venice; but unless their tastes have become wholly vitiated, unless their eyes are suffering from a surfeit of light, they will soon learn to find that their best beloved masters would not bear transplanting. They belong to the soil of the country they worked in, while Velazquez, like Rembrandt, can travel to any climate, and shine with unclouded glory in any atmosphere. It is impossible to imagine that Rubens could have painted with the palette that served Velazquez, but the greater of the two men has given the world an invaluable lesson in appreciation, and because Nature is full of exquisite colour harmonies that are quite subdued in tone it is well that we should have been taught to appreciate them. Velazquez himself declared that Raphael did not please him, but Titian did; he found in him the greatest of all the Venetians. And yet it is hard to say that he took anything from the admired master, because with Velazquez admiration and imitation are things apart. He did not even imitate El Greco, the painter whose influence upon the world of art is not yet fully acknowledged or understood, and he did not copy Rubens, whose splendours would have dazzled a weaker man.

Velazquez merely saw certain truths in Greco's handling of portraiture, and accepted them. Throughout his life he made a steady improvement in the quality of the work done, but the changes came through introspection rather than from any outside influence.

His pictures are divided by many critics into three styles, which may be divided roughly by his visits to Italy. In the early days the paint on his canvas was very thick, the shadows were heavy, the composition was not always conclusive or well devised. The one quality that was that irreproachable throughout all the years was the drawing, which was always masterly. From the days of the early "Bodegones" down to the "Meninãs" nobody could find a picture in which his drawing is obviously at fault; although in speaking of Velazquez it is of course difficult to separate drawing from painting. As he grew up the sense of composition and colour harmony became stronger and stronger, and the faults passed. At the same time, Velazquez was a severe critic of his own work, and a careful examination shows that even those pictures to which no suspicion can attach were retouched and corrected in the making.

In this country one secures little more than a glimpse of the master's work. The National Gallery has nearly a dozen pictures, but there are certain questions about the authenticity of some of them, and the Philip in the Dulwich Gallery is rather more than doubtful. The Wallace Collection has a few beautiful examples of Velazquez, and after that there are about fifty private owners of pictures that cannot be readily seen. Perhaps a considerable proportion of these works would, if subjected to very careful scrutiny, reveal themselves as copies by Mazo or others. In France there are half-a-dozen fine pictures in the Louvre. Germany can show some in Berlin, Dresden, and Munich; Holland has one or two. There are less than a dozen in all Italy. The Hermitage Gallery in St. Petersburg has five or six, and Vienna about twice as many; but to see Velazquez one must go to Madrid. The Museo del Prado has over sixty of the artist's pictures, and though a small proportion of these have scarcely a touch of the master's hand, all his greatest work has found a resting-place here. Las Lanzas, Las Hilanderas, Las Meniñas, Philip IV. on horseback, Don Balthasar Carlos on his pony, the Crucifixion, the Coronation of the Virgin, the Dwarfs, Æsop, Menippus—all these are to be seen in the Prado; the greater number being in the Salon of Isabella, an octagonal room in which one may spend long hours. The writer, on the occasion of his last visit to Madrid, made a note of the number of visitors to the famous octagonal room during the four mornings he spent there. In the course of some twelve hours the room was visited by some twelve people! It is only fair to say that it was not in the tourist season; the month was June, and nobody stayed in Madrid from choice.

PLATE VIII.—THE PRINCESS MARIA THERESA OF AUSTRIA

This daughter of Philip IV. became Queen of France. The picture was painted when she was about ten years of age, and consequently belongs to the last period of Velazquez' work. It was hung in the Alcazar until some time in the eighteenth century, when it was transferred to the Prado.

There are pictures by Velazquez to be seen in Madrid outside the Prado, but for the most part they are in private houses, and are not accessible to everybody. Seville boasts half-a-dozen canvases by her greatest painter, and there are a few elsewhere in Spain; but it may be said that those who know the Salon of Isabella have seen Velazquez at his best, and that those who have seen his other pictures and have not visited the Prado, do not know Velazquez at all.

Perhaps there are pleasant surprises yet in store for the art world, for many pictures are still untraced. Doubtless some have been destroyed by fire and others are in half-forgotten lumber rooms of palaces and galleries from which they will be gathered in due course. Velazquez owes a large part of his popularity in Spain to-day to the measure of appreciation he has secured beyond the borders. Every second-hand dealer in Madrid or Seville has a "genuine Murillo" to offer the stranger. It is worth a thousand pounds; but as the dealer is an honest man, he will sell it first for two hundred, then for one, and finally for fifteen or even ten. But no second-hand dealer shows a "genuine Velazquez." He knows that at best it could only appeal to artists, and he knows them for strange folk endowed with much enthusiasm, little money, and an embarrassing measure of knowledge of the methods by which genuine old masters are created to supply a long-felt want.

Milton Keynes UK
Ingram Content Group UK Ltd.
UKHW042146281024
450365UK00010B/669

9 789362 929280